Mary, the Girl who said Yes

Other books by Tom Molnar

Nonfiction

Jesus, Kind, Loving, Dangerous

Time Out for Happiness

The Joys of Science and Religion

The Universe of God and Humanity

Christianity, the Challenge
of a Changing World

Fiction (novels)

Swept Away

Dark Age Maiden

Tara's World

All available on Amazon

Mary, the Girl who said Yes

Tom Molnar

Apple Valley Press

Mary, the Girl who said Yes

Copyright 2013 © by Tom Molnar, updated 2026

ISBN 978-09766952–2-6

Scripture quotations are taken from the New Jerusalem Bible and the New American Bible.

Manufactured   in   the   United   States   of   America

Preface

Mary was only thirteen or fourteen, or at most, fifteen or sixteen. Yet in those days she was not a teen. The term "teenager" had not been invented. She was a woman.

And yet she **was** young. Quite young to be entrusted with the greatest work any woman has ever done. Was she looking forward to her wedding day, the day when she would be dressed like a queen and given to her husband, Joseph?

On such a day she and he would start a new life together. A life busy with much to do, plans to be made and future children to care for. A life lived among their people, with relatives, neighbors, tax collectors and the hated Roman soldiers who had defeated Israel and established their rule over the country.

To see the real Mary, we will go back to her time, when, like today, there was much going on and plenty to do. A time different than ours, a dangerous time, but filled with the same kinds of people: the wise and the foolish, the wealthy and the poor, and the humble and the proud. We will see the challenges she faced and the uncertainties that were part of her life as they are of ours. We will see a strong young woman, undaunted, who with trust in God, did what she had to do.

Mary has never sought acknowledgment for all she has accomplished. She gives credit only to God, and to her Son. She remains a person of great humility. As she said in her first conversation recorded in scripture, "Behold, I am the handmaid of the Lord. May it be done to me according to your word." (Luke 1:38)

Who was she really, this woman venerated as the mother of Jesus? So much has been written. Scholars delve into scripture, mystics see visions and Mary herself appears to some in apparitions. Who was this young Jewish girl who said yes to God? What was her life like? And why is she honored today by faith-filled Catholics, Protestants and Muslims? To learn more about her, we will start by looking at the typical Jewish household at the time she was born.

Contents

Chapter One

The birth of a daughter

Mary's birth, like that of all Hebrew children was a cause for joy. Her mother would be attended to by a midwife, and after delivery the child was cleaned, rubbed with a salt solution to toughen her skin, and wrapped in strips of cloth—swaddling clothes. Her father, who waited outside, often with other relatives, would hear her cry, and entering he would place the baby on his knee, the traditional manner in which the father of that day claimed the child as his own. Word of the birth of the new child quickly made the rounds of the village.

By Jewish law, Mary's mother was ritually unclean. She could not go into a synagogue to offer prayers for 80 days. For a son, 40 days was the period of waiting.

Mary, as was the typical Jewish custom, probably nursed for about two years. When she learned to walk, she usually stayed close to her mother. She learned to imitate her, and soon she learned to be of help. There was always plenty to do in a Jewish household.

What was her house like? The typical house at the time for any family, other than those well off, was made of clay, often supported by timbers. It was relatively small, with a door and only tiny windows or none at all. The inside of the house was fairly dark, even in full sunlight, and usually consisted of only one or two rooms.

The main room served all purposes. For sleeping, mats were laid on the hard packed earth floor. For eating, cushions or folded up mats provided seating around a low table. A single lamp, fueled by hand pressed olive oil, gave light. Cooking was often done outside, or in inclement weather, inside over a charcoal or wood fire. One side of the dwelling included a partition that separated the animals, often at a lower level, from the part of the house where the family lived. People in small towns and villages were usually quite dependant on their animals for both food and clothing.

The largest animal of a non-farming family was the donkey or ass. This beast of burden not only provided transportation, it also permitted the carrying of heavy items to and from the home. Other animals, goats and sheep supplied both milk and wool, from which it was the task of women to make clothing. Garments were few, as almost all were made at home. They were valuable, as may be noted that when Christ was crucified, the soldiers cast lots for his cloak. Knowing the cloak was valuable, even in the eyes of Roman soldiers, we may think of the long, long hours of work Mary put into the making of it.

At major feast times, particularly at the Passover, a lamb or goat would be slaughtered, one of the few times of the year when most families ate meat.

What do we actually know of the early life of Mary? A proto gospel, one of several gospels not recognized to be accurate, lists her parents as Joachim and Anne. It goes on to tell a pietistic story that Mary from the age of three lived her life in the temple, where she was fed by angels. At the age of twelve, the story continues, the temple officials needed to find a spouse for her to protect her virginity. Mary was highly esteemed and a large number of men wished to be her husband. They were told to leave their staffs in the temple for God to indicate to whom she should be espoused. As the story says, Joseph's staff sprouted flowers and a dove flew out of it. If you look at the statues of Joseph in many churches today, you may see his staff blooming.

The church does not recognize this gospel as genuine. Not only is the staff story hard to believe, there was no custom in Israel to have temple virgins dedicated to God. In fact, the opposite was true, only men were set aside to be priests and to preside in the temple.

We know enough about life in biblical times to describe the typical manner a Jewish child was raised. Mary's birth would have been a welcome cause for merriment, for the Jews loved children. If there is any truth to the proto gospel of James, she would have been especially welcomed, for barrenness in a wife was considered a cause for shame. Because the baby was female, not male, her mother would remain longer in an unclean state according to Jewish religious law. Her mother would have to wait eighty days before she could again enter the temple.

Once a daughter was trained, able to walk, and learning to talk she tended to follow in her mother's footsteps, much like today. If she had a baby brother or sister, she would learn childcare from her mother, and could practice with her own homemade doll, a toy popular among girls then as today. She would learn to treat her doll with care, imitating the care her mother gave her. Such has always been the way children learn, by following the example of the one who is closest to them.

The Nazareth that Mary grew up in was quite a small village; estimates range from 200 up to 500 people. The great majority of Nazoreans lived close to the land, and would have had to do for themselves the ordinary things we have come to take for granted. For example, they baked their own bread, made their own clothes, and without machines, washed them. Most other ordinary things they had to do for themselves. Mary would become proficient at doing these tasks at an early age.

Chapter Two

Mary, a girl of Nazareth

In Palestine there was much for a girl to learn how to do. According to Jewish law, a girl was considered to be marriageable at twelve and a half, so she needed to be able at a young age to carry out all the obligations of a woman.

Not all women were married by thirteen. Some were married later, the timing dependant on the initiative of her parents. Nevertheless, it was almost unseemly for a healthy young woman not to be married by eighteen. Most girls likely were espoused sometime between their thirteenth and fifteenth birthdays. We will learn more about that later.

Two of the main jobs women needed to be proficient at were meal preparation and making clothing. Both were much more difficult than today. Except in major towns, ready-made store bought goods were largely unavailable. One could purchase apparel in Rome and have it tailored to size, perhaps even in Jerusalem, but in smaller towns and villages, like Nazareth, that was not an option. Few villagers could afford ready made garments, and they would have simply not been a commodity one could purchase in a small town or village.

The same was true of food. In the smaller towns like Nazareth, one could buy the raw products for making meals, but even finding baked bread was unlikely. Bread was baked at home, almost every day.

At a young age, Mary would have seen her mother beginning the process of making bread. She would not have been able to help much then, for first the grain had to be ground. This was done by turning the heavy millstone on top of another stone with the kernels of wheat placed between them. Not easy work, certainly not a job a child could do until she grew stronger.

The gospel of Luke speaks of two women grinding together, with a peg set into the grinding stone so both could turn it together. It was sociable work, and women could chat while making a relatively hard job easier by cooperating at a common task. Once the kernels were ground into flour, water or goat's milk would be added along with olive oil and some yeast saved from the previous day. After kneading the bread and allowing it to rise, it was placed in a small home oven, often made of fired clay by a potter. Matches? There were no matches, so women tried to keep some embers glowing outside the house in warm weather and inside during the cold of winter. When it was time to bake or cook, the locally common broom shrub or tree provided thorns and wood often used for kindling. Then, the bread was set into the small ceramic oven.

Of course, people do not live by bread alone, although Hebrews considered their whole grain bread to be the main necessary ingredient for a meal. In a village like Nazareth there would be something like a "farmers market" where perhaps twice a week or more, one could purchase other ingredients for making meals. Olive oil was almost always in abundance and cheap. It was used not only for cooking but also as fuel for lamps. In Nazareth, and in all the towns near Lake Galilee, fresh or salted fish was usually available to buy. Most people ate fish far more often than meat.

Mary would have accompanied her mother to the market at an early age. Though it was only a short distance from their home, Mary as a little girl might have had a ride on the family beast of burden, the ass, a good sized donkey. She would have smelled the fishmonger's wares and peered into the large jars of wheat kernels, beans, lentils, and have seen colorful cloths laid on the ground, laden with all kinds of fruits, vegetables and berries in season. She would have seen the potter and his spinning wheel using different colors of clay to make various kinds of vessels for eating and drinking and for storage. Off to one side, within a corral, she would have seen and heard the braying of donkeys for sale—and also sheep, goats, young lambs, and perhaps poultry.

For a young girl, all the activity and people would likely have been exciting. She would have seen her mother bargaining with the vendors, trying to get a good price or leaving if the price was too high. Such was the way at Eastern bazaars then and to the present day. Westerners want a definite price, but Easterners enjoy the fun of trying to get the best bargain. Sometimes even the vendor will openly compliment a buyer if in their haggling back and forth he or she comes away with especially good value for their money.

Preparation for Marriage

In biblical times there were few occupations a Jewish woman could pursue. Her given career was to become a wife and mother, and if she happened to be barren, she would not be held in high esteem. In bible history, there are a few women who rose to eminence. For example, there is Judith, famous for beheading an enemy general whose forces threatened Israel, as well as Esther, who saved her people from execution, and Deborah, a prophetess and a judge.

Nevertheless, unlike today, the training of women focused on what she needed to know to be a good wife and mother. It is quite unlikely that Mary's training would have been any different. When she first appears in the Gospel of Luke, she is espoused to Joseph, which of course means that she and he will be married in due course.

Mary's age is not mentioned in the gospels, but we can guess at it with a fair amount of accuracy. That is because the normal age for a Jewish girl to be espoused in marriage was from twelve to sixteen. Usually the young man was a year or two older. With Joseph, a rather unreliable tradition has it that he was much older, in fact an elderly man.

It is likely that this belief began because of the doctrine held by the Catholic Church of Mary's perpetual virginity. The thinking seems to be that only an old man would have been able to live with a woman in a sexless union. However, that thinking may be completely off the mark. We know that carpentry work demands strength and agility, especially in a time when there were no power tools. We also know that Joseph lived for a minimum of twelve years after Christ was born, for he accompanied Mary and Christ to Jerusalem when Jesus was lost in the temple. In fact, after Christ began his public ministry at the age of thirty, he was referred to in Matthew, 13:55, as "the carpenter's son," which would appear to make it rather likely that Joseph's death came no more than a few years before Christ began his teaching.

For all the above reasons, and because in general life expectancy was much shorter than today, it is quite possible that Mary was espoused to a young man only a little older than herself. That was the norm in biblical times. We know that in those times parents made the choice about whom to marry, and, like any parents, Mary's would have wanted to find her a good man, one who could provide for and protect her and her future children. This was true then, even more so than today, for the biblical world was unfortunately a man's world, and an unattached woman had few rights. We may remember that Christ, even from the cross, gave Mary to be under the protection of the apostle John.

As mentioned, Mary first appears in the gospels as espoused to Joseph. It was the norm in Mary's time that the parents of two young people met and formally agreed that the youth and the girl were to become espoused. Ordinarily the parents knew each other and quite often the young man and woman were also familiar with each other. However, there was nothing then like the dating that is done today.

For the most part, people tended to marry within their class—that is, poorer families' children tended to marry those not well off, and wealthier families sought spouses for their children who also came from families of means.

In one way, we actually know more about Joseph's background than Mary's. He was trained and would make his living as a carpenter. As such, he could expect to enjoy a relatively secure middle class lifestyle which placed him far higher on the biblical social scale than laborers, shepherds and many others. His was a skilled occupation, and he would have been competent in using all the tools of the carpentry trade. His work would have tremendous variety, from erecting framework for houses, to making tables and furniture, to making and repairing farm implements, etc. It was not easy work, but it was work that was respected and necessary.

There is nothing in the Bible that refers specifically to the espousal of Mary and Joseph. However, there is plenty of historical information regarding the espousal process. Though it was the parents who made the arrangements, sometimes a youth might apprise his parents that he was interested in a particular girl.

Nazareth was the kind of small town where everyone knew everybody. This was true especially in that day, when walking was the only way to go to the synagogue, the market, to the well, or to the fields. It seems likely that a young man approaching marriageable age, then usually sixteen to eighteen, would take notice of the girls in his community.

However, during biblical times, it was practically forbidden for a man and woman to talk to each other except in the marketplace or while doing other business. A similar injunction exists today among traditional Muslim women. Nevertheless, in chance encounters about the small town, Joseph would have had the opportunity to take notice of Mary at the market or coming or leaving the synagogue, etc. He may even have done carpentry work for her family. Their eyes certainly may have met. We don't know, but it is entirely possible that Joseph could have asked his parents if they would arrange to have him espoused to a particular girl, Mary.

There is a big difference between espousal and engagement. In our day, a couple decides to become engaged and they may set a date for marriage. If they find they do not wish to continue their engagement, one or the other or both may break the engagement. There is no penalty other than hurt feelings and perhaps some embarrassment.

In biblical times, the betrothal of a man and woman was a formal agreement concluded by the parents or their representatives. A document was signed, a specific dowry to the family of the bride was settled, and a time for the marriage was set. In the eyes of the community, the couple was married, though not yet living together. If during the time before their marriage, the woman was found to be with the child of her espoused, the child would be accepted as a legitimate family member and heir.

However, if the woman should be caught in adultery, or should be conceived of a child not that of her espoused, she could be stoned to death. Even if she were not killed, it is most likely her espoused would have nothing to do with her, and a paper of divorce would be filed. Such was Mary and Joseph's situation after she was conceived of Christ in her womb.

Chapter Three

An angel visits Mary—The Annunciation

Mary's earliest appearance in the gospels is found in the gospel of Luke: ". . .the angel Gabriel was sent from God to a town of Galilee called Nazareth, to a woman betrothed to a man named Joseph, of the house of David, and the virgin's name was Mary."

Luke clearly states that Mary was "greatly troubled" by this visit, and by the angel's words, "Hail favored one, the Lord is with you."

The angel Gabriel subsequently told Mary, "You will conceive in your womb and bear a son, and you shall name him Jesus." Indicating what manner of man this was to be, the angel continued: "He will be great and will be called Son of the Most High, and the Lord God will give him the throne of David, his father, and he will rule over the house of Jacob forever, and of his kingdom there will be no end."

Mary did not understand the full meaning of what the angel was saying, for she asked, "How can this be, since I have no relations with a man?" To which Gabriel answered, "The Holy Spirit will come upon you, and the power of the Most High will overshadow you. Therefore, the child to be born will be called holy, the Son of God." Then the angel told her that her relative, Elizabeth, an older woman who was barren, was also with child, and now was in her sixth month, for "nothing is impossible for God."

Mary said to the angel, "Behold, I am the handmaid of the Lord. May it be done to me according to your word."

We don't know how soon after the angel's visit that she told Joseph of the event. We can only imagine his feeling of a trust violated. What could he think but that his espoused wife had been intimate with another man? By right, he could have had her stoned to death. Joseph's faith in humanity must have been shaken. Nevertheless, he decided to divorce her quietly rather than expose her to shame.

It was only after an angel of the Lord appeared to him in a dream that he decided not to end their betrothal. The angel's words, recorded in Matthew are: "Joseph, son of David, do not be afraid to take Mary your wife into your home. For it is through the holy Spirit that this child has been conceived in her. She will bear a son and you are to name him Jesus, because he will save his people from their sins."

Joseph heeded the angel's message and did not repudiate Mary. He knew that he as well as Mary would be the subject of gossip in the small town of Nazareth. Having a child before a couple officially lived together in marriage was not unheard of in biblical times, but it was certainly not as common as today. Such a child was, however, accepted as legitimate offspring of the betrothed couple. Nevertheless, for those in the small town who did not know the true nature of Mary's conception, and that would be everyone except Joseph and perhaps her parents, there was shame in carrying a child before the marriage ceremony.

Not too long after the angel's visit, Mary left town. She must have done so right away, for the angel told her that Elizabeth was "in her sixth month." Luke further specifies that Mary stayed with her relative for three months, probably until she delivered.

Mary had an important reason for visiting Elizabeth. She knew she had been barren, and that now God had acted directly in the life of the older woman to bring her a child. It is likely that Mary was filled with wonder and excitement at what God had wrought in her. She would be eager to express her delight to a woman also blessed by God. Besides, she could assist Elizabeth with demanding household tasks in the last months of her pregnancy.

How would Mary have traveled? By foot, almost certainly. Only the very wealthy, or small children on the backs of donkeys, were likely to travel in any other way. A very pregnant woman might be another exception to foot travel.

She traveled with a group. It was dangerous to go any other way. The roads were not policed, and the constant danger of bandits made group travel imperative. Mary did not have to wait long; people from Galilee frequently made the journey to Jerusalem, on business, or for the many Jewish Holy Days and observances. The trip itself would take days. Roughly seventy miles as the crow flies, the preferred route was longer but required less hill climbing. Much of it was along the Jordan River, which afforded fresh water for drinking and washing.

The caravan, the gathering of people traveling together, walked about ten to twenty miles a day. Consequently, they were on the road for at least several days, up to a week or more. Like the others, Mary would have taken the necessary provisions: a cloak for warmth, especially at night, a bag of relatively nonperishable food–like nuts, dried fruit, parched wheat and perhaps unleavened bread, and a jar or dried gourd for water. Camels were seldom used except for more long distance journeys, but hardy donkeys carried small children as well as any heavier items that needed to be transported to the destination.

The travelers stopped at times during the day to eat or rest, and at night, sometimes at inns, but at other times at a convenient spot away from the road. The inns were quite primitive, featuring a strong gate or door entering into a courtyard where the animals were kept. Water was provided for both animals and people and the better inns also had rooms to rent as well as a variety of food for sale.

Elizabeth and her husband Zachariah lived in a small hill town only a short distance from Jerusalem. Knowing that, and the fact that devout Jews sought to travel once a year to Jerusalem for the Passover, it is likely that Mary and her parents had visited Elizabeth and her husband Zachariah many times in the past.

Finally, after the long trip, Mary arrived at the outskirts of their house. Depending on the season of her travel, she would be dusty, or in the rainy season, have mud on her sandals. When she sees Elizabeth, the two women hurry to each other and embrace.

How old was Mary's relative? We should probably not think of her as elderly. She had been barren, yes. But such an appellation was given earlier than today. Jewish women were married early, as "teenagers." As previously noted, a girl was considered to be fully a woman by fourteen. With no contraception, and childless during her teens, twenties and even thirties, by her middle thirties if not before, a woman would sadly have been called "barren." Mary's older relative may have only been thirty-five, up to forty or so years of age, when God ended her curse of barrenness. Life was generally shorter then, though a few people did live to advanced years in biblical times. However, the average life expectancy for those living beyond childhood was apparently only in the fifties. This compares with calculations for Roman Empire life spans that averaged only fifty-two years.

Her baby, who would be named John, (St. John the Baptist), leapt in her womb and Elizabeth cried out, "Of all women you are the most blessed, and blessed is the fruit of your womb. Why should I be honored with a visit from the mother of my Lord? Look, the moment your greeting reached my ears, the child in my womb leapt for joy. Yes, blessed is she who believed that the promise made her by the Lord would be fulfilled." (Luke 1:42-45)

The Magnificat, or Canticle of Mary

We know Mary's answer to Elizabeth as recorded by Luke. He states: "And Mary said:"

"My soul proclaims the greatness of the Lord
And my spirit rejoices in God my Savior,
because he has looked on the humiliation of his servant.
Yes, from now onwards all generations will call me blessed,
For the Almighty has done great things for me.
Holy is his name,
and his faithful love extends age after age to those who fear him.
He has used the power of his arm,
he has routed the arrogant of heart.
He has pulled down princes from their thrones and raised high the lowly.
He has filled the starving with good things, sent the rich away empty.
He has come to the help of Israel his servant, mindful of his faithful love—according to the promise he made to our ancestors—of his mercy to Abraham and to his descendants for ever."

We should note, this is not the pious prayer of a contemplative. It is a forceful prophecy of Mary's own future and how the Lord will right the wrongs of those in power, bringing mercy to the poor and downtrodden as well as "faithful love" to those who follow Him.

Chapter Four

With high hope, a child is born

Although we know much about the lifestyle of people living in Israel, we know little of the personal life of Mary before she was visited by the angel Gabriel. We know that biblical Jews in the age of Christ were literate people, and the Bible was practically their only book, from which reading, writing, history, geography and law were studied. A devout young Jewish girl, Mary at an early age already knew much about the Old Testament. Scholars find great similarities in Mary's Magnificat with the words of Hannah in the Book of Samuel, and also in the words of several of the psalms. That Mary's words came from her own lips is the considered opinion of biblical scholars.

Mary stayed three months with Elizabeth, probably until her son, John the Baptist, was born. Then she returned home to Nazareth where she would likely have lived with her parents since she was not yet married.

In biblical times, the time of espousal was set, generally for one year but sometimes shorter. When the time of marriage arrived, there was great celebration. The bridegroom and his party of friends went, usually late at night, to the bride's house to take her to live in her husband's house. It was a huge event, even more so than current wedding celebrations. Everyone was dressed in their finest garments, sometimes borrowed, and the bride was prepared and dressed like a queen.

Since the bridegroom and his friends would usually come at a late hour, it was imperative that those virgins waiting, probably friends of the bride, have sufficient oil for their lamps. We should remember there were no flashlights in that day and no streetlights. To travel in the night without any illumination at all was dangerous because of uneven roads and numerous rocks. Jesus tells of the story of the five virgins who ran out of oil, (Matthew: 25), to illustrate the importance of being prepared for the kingdom of God.

Once the groom and his friends gathered the bride, she and her friends processed with them to the groom's house, or to a place where a feast would be set. There, in the ordinary course of events, after eating, drinking, and celebrating, the bride and groom would retire and consummate their union. The next day, and usually the next several days, the feasting and celebration would continue with music and plenty of wine. We will look later at how Mary asked Jesus to intervene at a wedding feast where they were running out of wine—a huge embarrassment for the groom and his family.

For Mary, there was likely no grand wedding celebration. After she returned from visiting Elizabeth she returned to live with her parents, every day growing larger with child. Soon, her pregnancy would become too large to conceal and then people would begin to talk. Devout Mary was with child. What a surprise! She and Joseph could not wait until the wedding. What a shame! Mary did not let the talk affect her. She had a bigger secret, one she could not tell her friends and neighbors. She was bearing the future king of Israel!

Mary remained humble. She knew that everything was done to her because of God, and not because of her. She went about her work in her family as before, grinding grain, making bread, carding wool, spinning and making clothing, tending the garden, going to get water at the well, etc. as well as talking with her friends and parents. In prayer, she waited patiently for her time.

Then came the news of the census. Joseph was required to go to Bethlehem as he was of the House of David. It is not certain that Mary also had to go. However she did go, despite being quite pregnant, trusting God in undertaking the long journey. Luke is specific in saying that Joseph went to Bethlehem ". . .to be enrolled with Mary, his **betrothed**, who was with child." It is clear from this that Mary and Joseph only began living together at this time.

Going to Bethlehem

The trip to Bethlehem was very similar to Mary's previous trip to visit her relative Elizabeth. About eighty miles. For the Jews at the time, the ass, or large donkey, was their beast of burden. Any family of means would have one to haul heavy things from the market or for a small child to ride on during a trip. Joseph, in particular, would have needed such an animal for hauling wood and the many things he made from wood. The pictures we see of Mary riding a donkey when they traveled to Bethlehem are probably accurate.

Bethlehem, the birthplace of David, was then a small town located only a few miles southwest of Jerusalem. The prophet Micah had foretold that a great ruler would come from Bethlehem, and that "his greatness shall reach to the ends of the earth." (Micah 5:2-3) Many Jews, and particularly Joseph and Mary, would have been aware of that prophecy, for like all Jews, they looked to a time when they would no longer be under the domination of Roman rule. Knowing that their son was destined to "rule over the house of Jacob forever," as told by the angel Gabriel, they may have seen the census in Bethlehem as a confirmation of their son's messianic future.

Regardless, the child to be born was not to receive a kingly welcome. Mary and Joseph came late to the small town of Bethlehem and found it filled with others like themselves, coming for the census. It is a misreading of scripture, however, to say that they were turned away at the inn.

Joseph had some relatives in Bethlehem, as he was of the house of David. Mary, too, had a relative, Elizabeth, whose home would have been only a few miles away from Bethlehem. The word, "inn," is translated from Greek in two different ways, but in this instance of Luke, it is the same word as the upper room Christ ordered for the last supper. It was, in reality, not an inn or hotel room, but a guest room. But the guest room was full, so there was no room for them there.

What did the relatives of Joseph do? They prepared a place for Mary and Joseph in either the storeroom or in the place for their animals. Many people of the time kept a few animals for their own use, like goats, a donkey or even an ox. Left outside during the day, in cold weather they were kept inside, in a place adjacent to or in the back of the main house. Mary and Joseph may well have preferred the privacy of the latter rather than giving birth in the crowded guest room.

When Jesus was born, probably with the aid of a midwife, the child was nursed and then wrapped tightly in swaddling clothes and laid in the manger. In biblical times, it was considered the right thing to do to wrap an infant in swaddling clothes. In fact, parents would be considered remiss if they did not. The cloth used was quite long, as much as fifteen or twenty feet and only two to four inches wide. Children were fairly tightly wrapped in the belief that this would make them grow straight and strong. As for the manger, it was actually a feeding trough for animals made out of wood to hold feed or hay.

Very soon, while Jesus was still in the manger, the shepherds came. The sheep tenders were in a nearby pasture keeping night watch over their flock when "the angel of the Lord appeared to them. . ." (Luke, 2:9). The angel was radiant with the glory of the Lord, and the shepherds were terrified. The heavenly visitor told them, "Do not be afraid. Look, I bring you news of great joy, a joy to be shared by the whole people. Today in the town of David a Savior has been born to you; he is Christ the Lord. And here is a sign for you: you will find a baby wrapped in swaddling clothes and lying in a manger."

The shepherds hastened into town and found Mary and Joseph with the baby Jesus lying in the manger. Excited that they had been favored to see the future king of the Jews, they repeated what the angel had told about Jesus. Everyone who heard them was astonished at what they said.

As for Mary, she too was deeply affected by the words of the shepherds. In fact, as Luke says, ". . .she treasured all these things and pondered them in her heart. (Luke 2:19)

Mary had much to think about. The virgin birth, as told to her by the angel Gabriel, had now come to be. The angel's words that her son would be "great," and "called the son of the Most High," gave Mary much to reflect on. The angel had also said that "he will rule over the house of Jacob and his reign will have no end."

Now, the visit of an angel to the shepherds announcing "… a Savior has been born to you; He is Christ the Lord," could only increase Mary's wonderment. Who, knowing anything of Jewish history, could have thought otherwise than that her son would become a glorious ruler of Israel, the savior of his people. However, the very next appearance of Mary, Joseph, and Jesus, as told in the Gospel of Luke, dramatically changed their expectations.

Chapter Five

Danger and violence

The occasion was the presentation in the temple. This event, also the second joyful mystery of the rosary, was not really so joyful. A typically Jewish observance, it marked the fortieth day after the birth of a firstborn son. In the book of Exodus God told Moses that all first born sons were to be consecrated to God.

So, Mary and Joseph came to the temple with Jesus and an offering of "a pair of turtle doves or two young pigeons." (Luke 2:24) We know that they would have come to the "Woman's Court," for while this part was open to all Jews, the inner temple was open only to men. There, they offered their gifts, and were met by Simeon, a righteous and devout man, as well as Anna, a prophetess.

Simeon had long waited to see the Messiah, and filled with the Holy Spirit, he took the baby Jesus in his arms and gave thanks to God:

"Now, Master, you are letting your servant go in peace as you promised; for my eyes have seen the salvation which you have made ready in the sight of the nations; a light of revelation for the gentiles and glory for your people Israel." (Luke 2:29-32)

Mary and Joseph marveled at the things being said about Jesus. Then Simeon blessed them, and speaking to Mary, added these words: "Behold, this child is destined for the fall and for the rise of many in Israel, destined to be a sign that is opposed—and a sword will pierce your soul too—so that the secret thoughts of many will be laid bare."

What Mary felt when she heard these words we do not know. Up to this time, she had learned only of her son's greatness as told to her by the angel Gabriel, and echoed by her relative Elizabeth, as well as the shepherds who heard the message of the heavenly hosts praising the birth of the Savior.

Now, for the first time, she came to know that the coming reign of her son would be opposed, and that she herself would suffer. Mary could not have known what was to come, nor could she know the magnitude of the opposition Jesus would face. As a faithful Jew, she would pray for strength to face whatever was to come, and leave the rest in the hands of God.

From this point on, Luke says nothing else about Christ's early days other than that the Holy Family returned to Nazareth. We rely on Matthew to tell us the dramatic events that happened next.

The first event was the visit by the Magi. Arriving from the "east," as described by Matthew, they had been following a star which apparently disappeared when they came to Jerusalem. They arrived at the palace of king Herod, probably assuming that if a new king was to be born, he would be born in the palace. Not finding him there, they asked where the newborn king of the Jews was to be found. King Herod, after consulting with his biblical authorities, told them that according to the prophecy of Micah, the Messiah was to be born in Bethlehem.

Matthew gives no time frame for the visit of the Magi, but from what follows, it is likely to have been months or even a year after Christ's birth. When the Magi came, the Holy Family was still living in Bethlehem, only a few miles south of Jerusalem. We don't know exactly why they had not returned to Nazareth, but a possibility is that knowing their son was to be the Messiah, they may have wanted to remain close to Jerusalem, the center of Jewish life.

According to Matthew, when the Magi left King Herod's palace the star they had been following reappeared and led them to where the Holy Family was staying. There they prostrated themselves before the baby, giving him homage and presenting their gifts of gold, frankincense and myrrh.

What would Mary and Joseph have thought, after seeing Jesus receive the homage from royal visitors from the east who likely had traveled nearly a thousand miles to reach their dwelling? Surely, that the angel Gabriel's message to her regarding this child of God was again validated.

However, their time of rejoicing was short, for that very night, an angel appeared to Joseph in a dream warning him that the murderous Herod was going to search for Jesus to destroy him. The angel told him to take Mary and the child to Egypt. In haste, he probably did so by early light of the following day. Fortunately they left in time, for soon after Herold sent his soldiers to slaughter all the children of Bethlehem who were two years old and under.

As Mary and Joseph made the long journey through the desert to Egypt, what must have been going through their minds? An innocent child is threatened with murder by a powerful king. Already, Mary comes to realize the unlimited hatred of evil as it impinges on the lives of her family, sending them far away to another country.

The journey would have taken many days, possibly weeks of travel on foot. Finally, on arriving, they likely would have been able to find the descendants of other Israelis who had not left Egypt at the time of the Exodus who could have given them food and temporary shelter. Then Joseph would have had to seek work using his carpentry skills and perhaps would have eventually built a house of his own for Mary and Jesus. By that time, word would have reached them of Herod's massacre of the innocents in Bethlehem and their prayers would go up to God that He had spared their son.

We don't know how long the Holy Family remained in Egypt, though some biblical scholars have suggested a year or longer. An angel again appeared to Joseph in a dream, telling him to return to Israel as king Herod was dead. However, they learned that Herod's son, Archelaus, was now in power, and decided to return to Nazareth, eighty miles distant from the seat of his power.

Chapter Six

A lost child—a wedding

For the next ten years, scripture is silent about the Holy Family. Jesus, like all Jewish youth, went to school in the synagogue and learned the history, the culture and the religious traditions of Judaism. He also learned the carpenter's trade, directly from his foster father. The stories and parables he would later tell show very well his perceptive understanding of life in a primarily rural community where farms, animals and fish played a major role in the day to day patterns of life. Nazareth was small, only a few hundred people, the kind of town where everybody knew everybody. For that reason, people didn't expect much from "the carpenter's son." Certainly not that the person they knew and grew up with was the long awaited Messiah.

The first indication that Jesus was special came in Jerusalem when he was twelve years old. Devout Jews arranged to go to Jerusalem every year. From Nazareth, it was an especially long trip, one that could have lasted as long as a week. Young children may have ridden on donkeys, but most people walked the entire distance, which, avoiding the hill country, was a journey about eighty miles long.

It was a happy time, and neighbors and relatives would travel together in large groups for companionship as well as to avoid robbers who sometimes preyed on single travelers. Children would band together, often laughing and playing games, and adults would enjoy discussing all manner of things and telling stories. At night, stopping sometimes at caravansaries or somewhere along the road, the sound of animated voices and perhaps music would subside until at last everyone went to sleep. Such was the nature of traveling to Jerusalem for Passover, to celebrate God saving his people from the bondage of Egypt.

It is not surprising, then, that twelve year old Jesus would not have been missed by his parents until they stopped for the night on their journey returning home. Luke tells us that they sought him among their relatives and friends. Not finding him, they became extremely upset. It is quite unlikely that they would have set off during the night, as with no light other than the stars and perhaps the moon, travel then would be both difficult and dangerous. Probably at the first light of morning they were hurriedly on their way, many hours later reaching Jerusalem and asking everyone if they had seen their son. Finally, after searching for yet another day, they found him—in the temple. He was seated in the midst of the teachers, listening and asking them questions.

Is it any wonder that Mary's words to Jesus were filled with the pain she had been experiencing? "My child, why have you done this to us? See how worried your father and I have been, looking for you. (Luke 2:48)

Jesus' answer was not exactly comforting to them. "Why were you looking for me? Did you not know that I must be in my Father's house?"

That Mary and Joseph did not understand what Jesus said to them is confirmed in Luke's gospel. He writes, "his mother kept all these things in her heart." Certainly, Mary was confused. She knew her son was to be the Messiah, the savior of Israel. Yet why did he seem to neglect her feelings? Especially as Luke tells us that afterwards "He went down with them and came to Nazareth and lived under their authority." (Luke 2:51)

We know from this incident and from other scriptural passages that Mary did not know the future in regard to her son. He could and did surprise her. As a good Jew, her heart was set on God and on her son. She didn't know the future, but in the fullness of time it would be revealed to her. In the meantime, she needed to trust and to have faith in the Lord.

We leave Mary's son now as a child and come to him next in the Gospels as a man. Joseph has died, we don't know when, but in Matthew Jesus is referred to by others as "the carpenter's son." From this, maybe it has not been too long since Joseph died before Christ began his ministry. The rest of the gospels of Mark, Matthew, Luke and John are concerned with Jesus. Mary is scarcely mentioned, with two important exceptions. The first has to do with Jesus' first miracle.

We remember it well, the wedding at Cana. A happy event, as previously noted, with the celebration usually lasting for days. Wine and good food in abundance were the usual necessities to bring merriment to the chosen guests. We can imagine the excitement of the wedding parties. The girl's friends, young, like herself, would be waiting for the bridegroom and his friends to come in the night to take the bride to his home, or perhaps to a larger place for the celebration.

They waited, with their lanterns lit, for they would also travel with them in the dark of night. The bride would be arrayed like a queen, bedecked with jewelry and even a crown in her hair; she would never dress finer than this night. The groom, too, would be resplendent like a king. As the girls waited, the tension would mount, until a shout told them that the groom's party had been heard or seen coming up the road. As the young man arrived, he formally took his new bride, and then all the young people would walk eagerly together to the party.

Cana is another small town in the Lake Galilee region, located a few miles north of Nazareth. Jesus was a guest as well as his mother. In fact, from the story, it may well be that Mary was an important relative to parents of the bride or groom. If so, she may have had something to do with the food and drink. John's gospel records that Jesus' disciples were also invited to the event, in which case it may not have been surprising that there was a shortage of wine.

Mary appears to be the first one to notice that they were running out of wine. She says to her son, "They have no wine."

Jesus answers her in a somewhat surprising way. "Woman, what do you want from me? My hour has not come yet." (John 2:4-5) There is much debate among scholars regarding Jesus calling his mother "woman." Certainly, it is not a negative term, but it may be that Jesus wanted Mary to know that he was no longer the son that she could always tell what to do. Interestingly, John records only one other time when Jesus called his mother woman—when he gave her to John from the cross.

Regardless, Mary knew her son better than anyone else, and she was not put off. Her next words were spoken to the stewards. "Do whatever he tells you to do."

We know what happened next. The story is told in John 2: 6-11. "There were six stone water jars standing there, meant for the ablutions that are customary among the Jews: each could hold twenty or thirty gallons. Jesus said to the servants, 'Fill the jars with water,' and they filled them to the brim. Then he said to them, 'Draw some out now and take it to the headwaiter.' They did this; the headwaiter tasted the water, and it had turned into wine. Having no idea where it came from—though the servants who had drawn the water knew—the headwaiter called the bridegroom and said, 'Everyone serves good wine first and the worse wine when the guests are well wined; but you have kept the best wine till now."

This was Christ's first public miracle, though it was known by only a few. It is significant that unlike so many of his other miracles, there was no major sickness or disease to be cured. It was done simply to save the embarrassment of the groom and his family. It was done because Mary asked her Son to help.

Jesus' apparent initial reluctance seems to indicate that he would not have performed the miracle except for the request of his mother. Jesus seems to make clear when he called her "woman" that Mary no longer had a mother's authority over him. Nevertheless, Jesus did perform the miracle, on his own authority, because it was the request of his mother. It can be seen from this that Mary, having no power of her own to work miracles, is able to come to the aid of those who invoke her intercession through the power of her son.

There are no other words recorded in scripture said by Mary. Yet Mary appears two more times in the gospels and again in the Acts of the Apostles. Though her speech is unrecorded, there is much we can learn from these appearances. For some important reason, we do not know why, Mary and some brothers and sisters (likely relatives) of Jesus come to see him. Jesus is inside, teaching to a houseful of people listening to his words. The message is passed to Jesus that "Your mother and brothers and sisters are outside asking for you." Jesus looks at those sitting in a circle around him and says, "Here are my mother and my brothers. Anyone who does the will of God, that person is my brother and sister and mother." (Mark 3:35)

Does Jesus refute his mother and relatives? Some may think so, but Jesus had a much higher purpose in mind. He extended his family to believers, to us as well, for as he said, "Anyone who does the will of God, that person is my brother and sister and mother."

Mary may very well not have understood what Jesus was saying at the time. What mother would? However, as she thought about it later, she would come to realize that the family Jesus was talking about was much larger than those who share his genes. It includes all those who believe in him. We too, are the brothers and sisters of Jesus—he has said so in this gospel. He has offered each of us to be members of his family. For Jesus, ties of faith are stronger than ties of family.

We next meet Mary at the foot of the cross. The prophecy of Simeon has come true: "a sword will pierce your soul too." Activity swirls around her, the soldiers, the crowd, the mocking of the pharisees, the words of those crucified alongside him. Her attention is fixed on Jesus alone, suffering above her. The son who would be the promised Messiah of Israel, who would "rule over the house of Jacob forever," as the angel Gabriel had told her. This is what it has come to—rejection by his own people and an ignominious and agonizing death on a cross. She trembles in her sorrow and John is there as are some women who have been close to Jesus. John helps her stand beneath the cross. Then Jesus speaks once again, this time looking down at Mary and John. "'Woman, behold thy son.' Then he said to the disciple, 'Behold your mother.' And from that hour the disciple took her into his home." (John 19:26-27)

Mary would have stayed to the end, despite the wind and the rain and the thunder and lightning. She witnessed the difficult work of removing the nails from his feet and hands to have him lowered once again into her arms as she sat on the ground to hold him for the last time. Her sorrow was utter and complete. They took Christ's body away for burial and John took her to his home.

Notwithstanding the gospel account, there is some tradition that Christ appeared first to his mother after His resurrection. However, we have it on no authority. It just seems right. So, though we have no further account of Mary in the gospels, she appears early on in the Acts of the Apostles.

Pieta, by Michelangelo

Chapter Seven

The hidden Mary

After the wedding at Cana, very little is spoken of Mary in the gospels. Even in the Acts of the Apostles, she is mentioned only once, as one of those disciples assembled waiting for the coming of the Holy Spirit. Only one evangelist, John, mentioned that she was at the cross. Why does Mary disappear from the record, and what do we know of her after Christ's death and resurrection?

One viewpoint regarding Mary's disappearance in scripture is that the apostles and Paul had much to say to initiate their listeners to Christ's message of salvation. The gentiles knew nothing of Christ, or even of Jewish tradition. To preach to the gentiles, the apostles needed to get across the message of salvation through Christ as simply as possible. Knowledge of Mary's role was not essential to their conversion.

Certainly, this analysis rings true, given the limited time the disciples had to bring the message of salvation to the world. However, it does not completely explain why Mary seems to practically disappear from the Gospels after Cana.

There may be a very good reason why Mary disappears from scripture. The gospels of Matthew, Mark and Luke were most likely written before the persecution of Nero, in 64 AD, and almost certainly before the destruction of Jerusalem by the Romans in 70 AD. That event, so tragically earth shaking for the Jews, is not mentioned in any gospel account. As for Mary, we do not know exactly when she died, but she was probably living when the first three gospels were written.

The major reason for the omission of Mary in scripture may well be that she was protected. Her son had been crucified, and by the time the gospels were written many of the apostles had been martyred. The religious authorities in Jerusalem wanted to eradicate Christians. We know their policy of stoning sinners, particularly women caught in adultery, and that they also stoned Stephen, the first Christian martyr, and many others. Paul was himself stoned, but left for dead and recovered. Mary too could have been stoned for conceiving out of wedlock.

Had they known her whereabouts, the authorities could have at any time seized Mary. They needed only to have asked a simple question of her, "Did you conceive your son Jesus by the Holy Spirit?" Mary would not have backed down, she would have answered "Yes," and the religious authorities would have accused her of blasphemy and then stoned her to death. It is a fact that, except for John, (and of course, Judas) every one of the original twelve apostles was martyred.

Consequently, there appears to be a very good reason why Mary is not mentioned at all in two gospels and very sparingly in the other two. John's gospel is the only one that shows that Mary was beneath the cross with Jesus, a striking omission in Mark, Matthew and Luke whose accounts are otherwise quite descriptive of the crucifixion. The reason? John's gospel was the last gospel written, and by that time Mary had died.

One could ask, from where did the evangelists get information on events relating to Mary? We believe Mary was alone when she was approached by the angel Gabriel. Similarly, few witnessed her visit to Elizabeth and only elderly Simeon and Anna, besides Joseph, were on hand to tell the story of the presentation of Jesus in the temple. Who else besides Joseph would remember the visit of the Magi and the rushed trip and stay in Egypt to escape Herod? We know Joseph was already dead before Christ's ministry started, when people would ask and want to know more about the early life of Jesus and Mary.

Who was it then that told these stories? It was Mary herself. So often, the gospels tell how Mary pondered things in her heart. The gospel of John describes the scene at the foot of the cross where Mary was given to the care of John.

What the gospel does not say, is that John himself is the beloved apostle, and that he is the one who took Mary into his home. Mary would have been quite comfortable with John. Though not known with complete certainty, it is likely that John's mother, Salome, who also was with Jesus beneath the cross, was a relative of Mary. Her sons, James and John, were the third and fourth disciples called by Jesus, and were probably with him at the wedding feast at Cana. John, along with his brother James, as well as Peter, were the apostles closest to Christ. They were also the apostles who were with him at his transfiguration and with him in the garden of Gethsemane.

John's first occupation was as a fisherman. He was not a poor fisherman, but one of the sons of Zebedee, who had a fishing business. That the business was doing well can be attested to by Mark's description of Jesus' calling of James and John. "At once he called them, and leaving their father Zebedee in the boat with the men he employed, they went after him." (Mark 1:20) It is apparent that Zebedee had a thriving business such that he employed others besides his two sons.

Was the business sold sometime after James and John left? We don't know, but we do know that Salome, their mother, was one of the women who was a follower of Christ. Mary would certainly have known her. Other women accompanied Jesus in his travels as both Mark and Luke describe:

"There were some women watching from a distance. Among them were Mary of Magdala, Mary who was the mother of James the younger and Joset, and Salome. These used to follow him and look after him when he was in Galilee. And many other women were there who had come up to Jerusalem with him." (Mark 15:40-41)

In Luke, 8:1-3, it is clear that women were part of Christ's entourage:

"Now it happened that after this he made his way through towns and villages preaching and proclaiming the good news of the kingdom of God. With him went the Twelve, as well as certain women who had been cured of evil spirits and ailments: Mary, surnamed the

Magdalene, from whom seven demons had gone out, Joanna the wife of Herod's steward Chuza, Susanna, and many others who provided for them out of their own resources."

However, let's get back to John and Mary. Mary is placed in John's care, and in time, her few belongings would have been moved to John's house, traditionally located on Mount Zion, just outside the walls of the old city of Jerusalem. John's mother, Salome, may also have lived there, at least while they were waiting for the coming of the Holy Spirit.

During the time Mary lived in his house, including when he moved to Ephesus, John would have learned first hand of all the things Mary had stored in her memory about Jesus. It is likely that many of Christ's followers, including the other apostles, would also have taken time to visit Mary and learn from her more about the early life of Jesus.

Did John actually write the Gospel of John? Scholars have different opinions. Even if John was only sixteen or seventeen when he left home to follow Jesus, he would have been near eighty or older by the time the gospel was written. Certainly, as the only surviving apostle, John would have had devoted followers holding on to every word he could tell them about Jesus. Consequently, if John himself did not actually write his gospel, one of his close followers did; for John's description of actual places and events in Jerusalem and Galilee leave no doubt that his gospel is an eyewitness account.

Chapter Eight

Apparitions of Mary and Guadalupe

Since Christ walked the earth, teaching a selfless love for both God and man, Christianity has continued to grow throughout the world. Mary, too, has continued to grow in influence and stature. Jesus has honored His mother, giving her a role to play in the salvation of many. Early on in church history there are records of her appearances on behalf of the message of God. In more modern times, some of her apparitions have been approved not only by the local bishop, but also by the Vatican. Though Mary's appearances are not part of the dogma of either Catholic or Protestant Churches, some of them have had a major historical impact affecting the lives of countless millions of people. We will consider a few of the fully approved major apparitions of Mary.

Mary's words in major apparitions

Although there have been hundreds of recorded Marian apparitions, the number that have been officially approved by both the local bishop and the Vatican have been quite small. The Catholic Church, through her bishops and the pope, has been very careful in verification of authenticity. Yet even among those that have been officially approved, there is no obligation for Catholics or Protestants to believe them. They are not officially part of the Catholic Church's depository of beliefs.

Nevertheless, many of the Marian apparitions have had a tremendous impact, and some of the places where Mary has appeared continue to be sites of ongoing miraculous cures. Those who are cognizant of the personal love of Mary and her son see her continued solicitude for the children of God as important for us and the church. What exactly does Mary say in her appearances, and what is their historical significance?

We will focus on only four. In reality, there are only sixteen that are Vatican approved in the last five hundred years. By far the oldest is the appearance of Our Lady of Guadalupe to Juan Diego in December, 1531 on a hill currently within Mexico City. Omitting Juan Diego's replies to her, we have less than 800 words that Mary spoke to him. Yet, with the exception of Fatima, this appears to be her longest discourse.

Guadalupe

Juan Diego, now a saint, was 57 years old when Our Lady appeared to him. Notice the words Mary uses when she talks to him.

"Jaunito, dearest Juan Diego."

"Listen, Juan, my dearest and youngest son, where are you going?"

"Know, know for sure, my dearest, littlest, and youngest son, that I am the perfect and ever Virgin Holy Mary, Mother of the God of truth through Whom everything lives, the Lord of all things near us, the Lord of heaven and earth. I want very much to have a little house built here for me, in which I will show Him, I will exalt Him and make Him manifest. I will give Him to the people in all my personal love, in my compassion, in my help, in my protection: because I am truly your merciful Mother, yours and all the people who live united in this land and of all the other people of different ancestries, my lovers, who love me, those who seek me, those who trust in me. Here I will hear their weeping, their complaints and heal all their sorrows, hardships and sufferings. And to bring about what my compassionate and merciful concern is trying to achieve, you must go to the residence of the Bishop of Mexico and tell him that I sent you here to show him how strongly I wish him to build me a temple here on the plain; you will report to him exactly all you have seen, admired and what you have heard. Know for sure I will appreciate it very much, be grateful and will reward you. And you? You will deserve very much the reward I will give you for your fatigue, the work and trouble that my mission will cause you. Now my dearest son, you have heard my breath, my word; go now and put forth your best effort."

[Juan Diego then went to the bishop as Mary had told him. The bishop did not believe him, and Juan returned to where he had seen Our Lady. When she appears, he tells her that she should send someone more important than him.]

"Listen to me, my youngest and dearest son, know for sure that I do not lack servants and messengers to whom I can give the task of carrying out my will. But it is very necessary that you plead my cause and, with your help and through your mediation, that my will be fulfilled. My youngest and dearest son, I urge and firmly order you to go to the bishop again tomorrow. Tell him in my name and make him fully understand my intention that he start work on the chapel I'm requesting. Tell him that I am the ever Virgin, Holy Mary, the Mother of God, who is sending you."

[Juan Diego went again to the bishop, and as he still didn't believe, he returned again to the same place where he saw Mary.]

"That is fine, my youngest and dearest son; you will return here tomorrow so that you may take the sign he asked for. Then, he will believe and no longer doubt or be suspicious of you; and know, my dear son, I shall reward your care, work and fatigue in my behalf. Go now."

[Juan learns his uncle is deathly sick with the plague. He is very concerned for him and is in a hurry to find a priest to give him last rites. So, instead of going to the place where Mary appeared to him, he goes to the other side of the hill on his way to find a priest. He is trying to escape Mary. Mary, however, appears to him there.]

"What is happening, dearest and youngest of my sons? Where are you going? Where are you headed? Listen, put it into your heart, my youngest and dearest son, that the thing that disturbs you, the thing that afflicts you, is nothing. Do not let your countenance, your heart be disturbed. Do not fear this sickness of your uncle or any other sickness, nor anything that is sharp or hurtful. Am I not here, I, who am your Mother? Are you not under my shadow and protection? Am I not the source of your joy? Are you not in the hollow of my mantle, in the crossing of my arms? Do you need anything more? Let nothing else worry you, disturb you. Do not let your uncle's illness worry you, because he will not die now. You may be certain that he is already well."

"Go up, my dearest son, to the top of the hill, to where you saw me and received my directions and you will find different kinds of flowers. Cut them, gather them, put them all together, then come down here and bring them before me."

"My youngest and dearest son, these different kinds of flowers are the proof, the sign that you will take to the bishop. You will tell him from me that he is to see in them my desire, and therefore he is to carry out my wish, my will. And you, who are my messenger, in you I place my absolute trust. I strictly order you not to unfold your tilma or reveal its contents until you are in his presence. You will relate to him everything very carefully: how I sent you to the top of the hill to cut and gather flowers, all you saw and marveled at in order to convince the Governing Priest so that he will then do what lies within his responsibility so that my house of God which I requested will be made, will be built."

[This time, when Juan Diego went back, the bishop believed, for when he opened his cloak to show the fresh flowers, the image of the virgin appeared on his cloak. The bishop and his attendants knelt down in homage to Mary.]

The significance of Guadalupe cannot be underestimated. The Spanish had defeated the Aztecs ten years before, ending their practice of human sacrifice, and a number of missionaries labored to bring native Indians to the faith. Some accepted, like Juan Diego himself, but most Indians saw the coming of the Spanish as a two edged sword. On the one hand, they ruled over them, forcing many to work in the gold mines, and on the other, their missionaries sought to bring them to faith in Jesus.

Mary's appearance in the garb of an Indian maiden, speaking to Juan Diego in his native tongue, had a tremendous impact. The Indians now saw that the mother of God was like them, a person who cared for them and their culture. Within a matter of years, millions of native peoples became Christian. Today, inspired by Guadalupe, Mexico and most of Latin America are Catholic countries.

The original tilma, or cloak of Juan Diego is still on display in the Basilica of Guadalupe in Mexico City. It is made of cactus fiber, the cloth of the poor in sixteenth century Mexico. Though it should have decayed in a few decades it has been miraculously preserved for 500 years. The image of Mary on Juan Diego's cloak in the Basilica is venerated by millions of people every year.

Painting of Mary and Saint Juan Diego

Chapter Nine

Lourdes

Mary's appearance to fourteen year old Bernadette Soubirous in February of 1858 set off a chain of events of continuing importance. Bernadette was the oldest of nine children, although four of them died at an early age. Bernadette's family had become impoverished. Her father was a miller, grinding grain for the farmers, but two years of parched crops and the startup of a new coal powered mill had ruined his business. The whole family now lived in a one-room dwelling.

On the day of the apparition, Bernadette's mother told her children that they had run out of wood to burn at the hearth. Bernadette and one of her sisters, as well as a friend of theirs, went to the nearby river to gather firewood. Bernadette lagged behind the other two, as they crossed the shallow water to get to the other side. She heard a sudden wind blowing, and then saw a small golden cloud emerging from an opening in a large cave. Then an "exceedingly beautiful" young girl appeared. The girl looked at Bernadette, smiled, and motioned for her to come closer.

Bernadette was later questioned interminably by various officials and churchmen. Asking about Mary's appearance, she told them this: The lady had the appearance of "a young girl, sixteen, or seventeen years old. She wore a white dress drawn in at the waist by a blue ribbon whose ends hung down. On her head she wore a long white veil so as almost to cover her hair. Her feet were bare but nearly covered by the folds of her dress, except at the tip where a yellow rose shone on each. On her right arm she carried a rosary of white beads on a golden chain, shining like the roses on her feet."

Mary appeared to Bernadette a total of eighteen times in the late winter and early spring of 1858. Crowds began to gather hoping to see what Bernadette saw. At first a few and later over a thousand came. None of them were able to see the Virgin Mary that Bernadette described. In many of the appearances that Mary made to Bernadette she was silent, sometimes only smiling and at other times without words saying the rosary with her. The beads she carried moved as they prayed together. Below is the sum total of Mary's words. There are some slight variations recorded, but the account below seems accurate and does not show the minor elaborations shown in some of the other accounts.

"It is not necessary." On being offered pen and paper by Bernadette (villagers had coerced Bernadette to ask for this.)

"Would you have the graciousness to come here for fifteen days? I do not promise you happiness in this world, but in the next."

"Pray for sinners."
"Go drink at the spring and wash yourself in it."
"Penance! Penance! Penance!"

[When Mary told Bernadette to drink and wash at the "spring," there was only a puddle of muddy water within the cave. Bernadette tried to comply, and as she groveled in the mud, clear water began to flow in quantity. It has continued to flow from that day until today.]

Mary reiterated her request for a chapel to be built and also said that people should come to the grotto in procession. In one of her appearances, she explained to Bernadette that she had not come the evening before because, in her own words, "There were people here who wanted to see your face in my presence, and they were unworthy of it. They spent the night at the grotto and profaned it."

"I am the Immaculate Conception."

"I am the Immaculate Conception." were Mary's last words.

What has been the significance of this apparition? Many people are aware of the continuing cures that began immediately and have continued to this day. Although many thousands of cures have been documented, only 67 have been officially recognized as miracles by the Catholic Church. There are reasons for this. For one, the illness must be serious and the cure must be sudden and complete. There must be no need for convalescence. Furthermore, no regular medication that might eventually effect a cure may have been taken, and the cure must be beyond the prognosis for the particular disease or condition.

Other safeguards, such as personality assessments, are used to rule out false claims, illusion and hysteria. Certainly, there are many genuine cures that occur that are simply not brought to the International Medical Committee besides those that do not meet their strict guidelines. Probably far more numerous are spiritual cures that involve a change of heart and a turning toward God. Lourdes continues to be a popular destination for Catholics and Protestants, as well as others. The small French town of only 15,000 people has approximately 270 hotels and averages five million visitors a year.

Chapter Ten

Fatima

It is likely that most people have heard of Fatima, though the amazing and appalling events that happened there are not as well known. The small town is in the middle of Portugal, a country about the size of the state of Indiana. This account presents all the recorded words of Mary as before, but to understand them we need to include what was happening as well as the words of Lucia, whose questions Mary frequently answered. Lucia was the oldest of three children, all of whom saw the appearances of Mary.

May 13th, 1917

When about halfway down the slope, there was another flash of light, and a lady appeared above a holm-oak tree. Lucy says that the lady was "all dressed in white, more brilliant than the sun, radiating a light clearer and more intense than a crystal glass filled with clear water pierced by the most burning rays of the sun." The children stopped and found themselves in the light that emanated from Her.

Lucy describes the apparition in this way:
"Then Our Lady said to us, **'Do not be afraid. I will do you no harm.'**
'Where is Your Grace from?' I asked Her.
'I am of heaven.'
'What does Your Grace want of me?'
'I have come to ask you to come here for six months in succession, on the 13th day, at this same hour. Later on, I will tell you who I am and what I want. Afterwards, I will return here yet a seventh time.'
'Shall I go to heaven too?'
'Yes, you will.'
'And Jacinta?'
'Also.'
'And Francisco?'
'Also, but he will have to say many rosaries.'
Lucia asks about two girls who had died recently.
'Is Maria das Neves already in Heaven?'
'Yes, she is.'
'And Amelia?'
'She will be in purgatory until the end of the world.'
'Are you willing to offer yourselves to God to bear all the sufferings He wants to send you, as an act of reparation for the sins by which He is offended, and for the conversion of sinners?'
'Yes, we are willing.'
'You are then going to have much to suffer, but the grace of God will be your comfort.'

Mary at that point opened her hands and the children experienced a strong light '. . .it made us see ourselves in God, . . .' The children fell to their knees in adoration of God.

'Recite the rosary every day in order to obtain peace for the world and the end of war.' [World War I was being fought.]

Lucia asks, 'Can you tell me whether the war will still last a long time, or if it will soon end?'

'I cannot tell you yet, as I have not yet told you what I want.'

Perhaps it should be said, that during all the apparitions, only Lucia spoke to Our Lady. Jacinta heard her, but did not speak, and Francisco saw her but did not hear and so the girls had to tell him afterwards what she said.

June 13th, 1917

Mary appears at the same place as the month before, and Lucia asks: 'What does your grace want of me?'

'I want you to come here on the 13th of next month, to pray the rosary every day, and to learn how to read. Later I will tell you what I want.'

Lucia asks for the cure of a sick person.

'If he is converted, he will be cured within the year.'

'I would like to ask you to take us to heaven.'

Yes, I will take Jacinta and Francisco soon, but you, Lucy, are to stay here some time longer. Jesus wishes to make use of you in order to make me known and loved. He wishes to establish in the world devotion to my Immaculate Heart. To whoever embraces this devotion, I promise

salvation; those souls will be cherished by God, as flowers placed by me to adorn His throne.'

'Am I to stay here alone?'[Lucia is sad she alone has to stay on earth.]

'No, my daughter. Are you suffering a great deal? Do not lose heart, I will never forsake you! My Immaculate Heart will be your refuge and the way that will lead you to God.'

Mary then showed them a heart, held in her right hand, surrounded by thorns.

July 13th, 1917

By this third apparition, a crowd of several thousand people had gathered in waiting. Lucia led them in the rosary. Then, preceded by a flash as of lightning, Mary appeared.

'What does your grace want of me?'

'I want you to come here on the 13th of next month, to continue reciting the rosary every day in honor of Our Lady of the Rosary, in order to obtain peace in the world and the end of the war, because only she can help you.'

Lucia says, 'I should like to ask you to tell us who you are, and to work a miracle so that everyone will believe that your Grace is appearing to us.'

'Continue to come here every month. In October, I will say who I am and what I want, and I will perform a miracle so that all might see and believe.'

'Sacrifice yourselves for sinners, and say often to Jesus, especially whenever you make a sacrifice: O Jesus, it is for love of Thee, for the conversion of sinners, and in reparation for the sins committed against the Immaculate Heart of Mary.'

The vision of hell [As told by Lucia, who had become a nun, written many years later.]

"As Our Lady spoke these last words, she opened Her hands once more, as she had done during the two previous months. The rays of light seemed to penetrate the earth, and we saw as it were a sea of fire. Plunged in this fire were demons and souls in human form, like transparent burning embers, all blackened or burnished bronze, floating about in the conflagration, now raised into the air by the flames that issued from within themselves together with great clouds of smoke, now falling back on every side like sparks in huge fires, without weight or equilibrium, amid shrieks and groans of pain and despair, which horrified us and made us tremble with fear. (It must have been this sight which caused me to cry out, as people say they heard me.) The demons could be distinguished by their terrifying and repellent likeness to frightful and unknown animals, black and transparent like burning coals. That vision lasted only a moment, thanks to our good Mother of Heaven, Who, at the first apparition, had promised to bring us to Heaven. Without that, I think we would have died of terror and fear.
Terrified and as if to plead for succor, we looked up at Our Lady, who said to us, so kindly and so sadly:

> **'You have seen hell where the souls of poor sinners go. To save them, God wishes to establish in the world devotion to My Immaculate Heart. If what I say to you is done, many souls will be saved and there will be peace. The war is going to end; but if people do not cease offending God, a worse**

one will break out during the reign of Pius XI. When you see a night illumined by an unknown light, know that this is the great sign given you by God that he is about to punish the world for its crimes by means of war, famine, and persecutions of the Church and of the Holy Father.

'To prevent this, I shall come to ask for the consecration of Russia to My Immaculate Heart, and the Communion of Reparation on the First Saturdays. If My requests are heeded, Russia will be converted and there will be peace; if not, she will spread her errors throughout the world, causing wars and persecutions of the Church. The good will be martyred, the Holy Father will have much to suffer, various nations will be annihilated. In the end, My Immaculate Heart will triumph. The Holy Father will consecrate Russia to Me, and she will be converted, and a period of peace will be granted to the world. In Portugal, the dogma of the Faith will always be preserved. Do not tell this to anybody. Francisco, yes, you may tell him.

'When you pray the Rosary, say after each mystery: O my Jesus, forgive us, save us from the fires of hell. Lead all souls to heaven, especially those who are most in need.'

After a moment of silence, Lucia asked, 'Is there anything else that you want of me?'

'No, I do not want anything more of you today.'

August 13th and 19th, 1917

Kidnapped!

On August 13th, somewhere between 10,000 and 20,000 people gathered to wait for the next apparition. However, the children were not there. They were in jail.

They had been seized by the mayor of the county, Artur Oliveira Santos, a baptized Catholic who at the age of twenty had left the church to join the Masonic Lodge. Not only did he have political power, he was also the publisher of a newspaper which sought to undermine the faith of the people. Realizing that the apparitions were drawing huge crowds and reviving faith, he sought to end them in any way possible.

To do that, he intercepted the children as they were on their way to see Mary. He encouraged them to ride with him to the site of the apparitions. Veering away from the site, he put the children, aged ten, nine and seven, into a jail with criminals. Santos interrogated them at length, together and separately, trying to find out the secrets of Fatima. In his interrogations of these young children, Santos focused on trying to learn the first secret of Fatima, of which Mary had told them not to reveal. Not getting anywhere with all his questioning, he resorted to a most inhuman scheme. He told them he would boil them in oil.

A huge vat of oil was prepared, and asking the children again of the secret, he took the youngest, seven year old Jacinta, into another room to be fried in oil until dead. Next, he questioned Francisco, telling him he would be the next to meet the same fate as his sister. Francisco bravely refused to reveal the secret, and was taken away to meet a horrible death. Last, Santos gave the ultimatum to Lucia, who, thinking her cousins had been killed, gave herself to be boiled to death in oil. Santos' threat was not carried out, and at last the children were reunited.

Santos was beaten by the courage of the children. Taking them again in his carriage, he left them off within walking distance of their homes, driving off quickly so as not to incur the wrath of the villagers.

With none of the children there to witness the apparition on the 13th, something nevertheless happened. A witness to the scene reported hearing a clap of thunder and seeing a small white cloud which hovered at the usual place of Mary's appearance. The grass beneath them, their clothing, and their faces shimmered with different colors as had happened before during the heavenly visits. On the 19th, when the children went to put their sheep out to pasture, Our Lady again appeared to them.

Lucia asked, 'What does your Grace want from me?'

'I want you to continue going to the Cova da Iria on the 13th, that you continue praying the Rosary every day. On the last month, I will perform a miracle so that all may believe. If they had not taken you to the town, the miracle would have been greater. Saint Joseph will come with the Child Jesus, to give peace to the world. Our Lord will come to

bless the people. Our Lady of the Rosary and Our Lady of Sorrows will come also.'

'What do you want them to do with the money the people leave at the Cova da Iria?'
'Have two litters made. You will carry one with Jacinta and two other girls dressed in white; the other one Francisco is to carry, with three boys, like him, dressed in white. It will be for the Feast of Our Lady of the Rosary. What is left over will help toward the construction of a chapel that is to be built.'
'I should like to ask you to cure some sick persons.'
'Yes, I will cure some of them during the year.'
'Pray, pray very much, and make sacrifices for sinners, for many souls go to hell because they have no one to make sacrifices and pray for them.'

September 13th, 1917

An even larger crowd gathered, as Lucia later wrote, "... as many as thirty thousand people"
'What does your Grace want of me?'
'Continue to pray the rosary in order to obtain the end of the war. In October, Our Lord will come as well as Our Lady of Sorrows and our Lady of Mount Carmel, and Saint Joseph will appear with the Child Jesus in order to bless the world. God is satisfied with your sacrifices, but He does not want you to sleep with the rope. Wear it only during the day.'

[The children had taken to wearing a tight rope around their waists under their clothes as a penance.] Then Lucia asked for some cures.

'I shall cure some, but others no, because Our Lord does not trust them.'

Lucia says, 'The people would indeed like to have a chapel here.'

'With half the money received so far, they should make litters and carry them on the Feast of Our Lady of the rosary; the other half can be used to build the chapel.'

Lucia then offered Our Lady two letters and a flask of fragrant water given to her by others.

'This is not suitable for heaven. In October I will perform the miracle so that all may believe.'

October 13th, 1917

This time a huge crowd, estimated at 70,000 people, came on a cold rain soaked day, gathering on the muddy ground of the Cova da Iria. When Our Lady appeared, Lucia, as always, began the conversation.

'What does Your Grace want of me?'

'I want to tell you that a chapel is to be built here in my honor. I am the Lady of the Rosary. May you continue always to pray the Rosary every day. The war is going to end and the soldiers will soon return to their homes.'

'I had many things to ask you: to cure some sick people, to convert some sinners, etc.'

'Some yes, others no. They must amend their lives and ask pardon for their sins. Do not offend the Lord Our God any more, for He is already too much offended!'

'You want nothing more from me?'

'No, I want nothing more from you.'

Lucia shouted, 'She is going! She is going! Look at the sun!'

The sun then began its spectacular movements, witnessed by the whole crowd. A few eyewitness accounts, listed below, tell the story.

"The sun turned like a fire wheel, taking on all the colors of the rainbow." (Maria da Capelinha)

"We suddenly heard a clamor, like a cry of anguish of that entire crowd. The sun, in fact, keeping its rapid movement of rotation, seemed to free itself from the firmament and, blood-red, to plunge toward the earth, threatening to crush us with its fiery mass Those were some terrifying seconds." (Dr. Almeida Garrett)

"From those thousands of mouths I heard shouts of joy and love to the Most Holy Virgin. And then I believed. I had the certainty of not having been the victim of a suggestion. I had seen the sun as I would never see it again." (Mario Godinho, an engineer)

Many reports also describe another lesser miracle. After the sun's display, the muddy ground suddenly dried, and the rain drenched clothes of the people were completely dry.

Mary told the children that the first World War would end but said that a second, worse World War would come if Russia was not converted. She foretold that all the struggles, genocide and destruction of World War II could have been avoided by answering her worldwide plea for prayers, sacrifices and praying the rosary. Her message seems to indicate that more wars, famines and persecutions will not end until her message is heard and put into practice.

Chapter Eleven

The rosary, a different kind of prayer

The rosary, the prayer Mary wants her "children" to pray, is an interesting and in some ways an unusual devotion. Far from being rote repetition, it is a means of meditation, and one historically used by kings, bishops and peasants.

The beads do form its outline, but they only open the door to its possibilities. There is a reason why the rosary is prayed by popes, clergy, and ordinary men and women everywhere.

The rosary is composed of the common prayers of the church. Its focus is on Jesus, Mary and God the Father. Before showing how the rosary is actually prayed, we will list the individual prayers, because not everyone knows how they originated and their wording.

An Our Father initiates each of the ten Hail Mary's. We know where the Our Father comes from: from Our Lord himself. In the gospel of Matthew, 6:9-13 and a slightly shorter version in Luke, 11: 2-4.

Where does the Hail Mary come from? The first part is the greeting of the angel Gabriel, from the gospel of Luke: "Hail, favored one! The Lord is with you." (Luke, 1:28) The second line comes from Mary's relative, Elizabeth: "Most blessed are you among women, and blessed is the fruit of your womb." (Luke, 1:42)

The last line of the prayer, "Holy Mary, mother of God, pray for us now and at the hour of our death," was added later. Historians don't know exactly when, but it was used in the Middle Ages, and was made official in the catechism of the Council of Trent in 1566. Significantly, this last part asks for Mary to pray for us, not for her to do something for us. Only God can do something for us, but faithful Christians frequently ask others to pray for them. Particularly in time of need. As the person closest to Jesus, Mary's prayer for us is particularly powerful.

Two other prayers, included within the rosary, but also said separately are the Apostles' Creed and the Glory Be to The Father. Both of these have a long history. The Apostles' Creed is a shorter version of the Nicene Creed, which states the major beliefs of Christianity and became official with the Council of Nicea in 325 AD. The Glory Be to The Father prayer also had a very early beginning and affirms the Trinitarian nature of God the Father, Son, and Holy Spirit.

The following are the words to the prayers of the rosary:

Hail Mary

Hail Mary,
Full of Grace
The Lord is with you. (or thee)
Blessed art thou among women,
and blessed is the fruit
of thy womb, Jesus.
Holy Mary,
Mother of God,
pray for us sinners now,
and at the hour of our death.
Amen.

The Our Father

Our Father, Who art in heaven,
Hallowed be Thy name.
Thy kingdom come.
Thy will be done, on earth as it is in heaven.
Give us this day our daily bread.
And forgive us our trespasses,
as we forgive those who trespass against us.
And lead us not into temptation,
but deliver us from evil. Amen.

The Apostles' Creed

I believe in God, the Father Almighty, Creator of heaven and earth; and in Jesus Christ, His only Son, Our Lord, Who was conceived by the Holy Spirit, born of the Virgin Mary, suffered under Pontius Pilate, was crucified; died, and was buried. He descended into hell; the third day He rose again from the dead; He ascended into heaven, sits at the right hand of God the Father Almighty; from thence He shall come to judge the living and the dead. I believe in the Holy Spirit, the holy catholic (or universal) Church, the communion of saints, the forgiveness of sins, the resurrection of the body, and life everlasting. Amen.

[The word catholic is translated from Greek and means universal, or universal church. Since the Middle Ages the term has been capitalized, as Roman Catholic Church. Those faithful who are not of this church may wish to use universal instead.]

Glory Be To The Father

Glory be to the Father, and to the Son, and to the Holy Spirit, as it was in the beginning, is now, and ever shall be, world without end. Amen.

Two additional prayers

The Hail Holy Queen prayer is ordinarily said at the end of the rosary. Some prefer the Memorare. Both prayers can be said at any time apart from the rosary.

Hail, Holy Queen

Hail, holy Queen, Mother of mercy, hail, our life, our sweetness and our hope. To thee do we cry, poor banished children of Eve: to thee do we send up our sighs, mourning and weeping in this vale of tears. Turn then, most gracious Advocate, thine eyes of mercy toward
us, and after this our exile, show unto us the blessed fruit of thy womb, Jesus, O merciful, O loving, O sweet Virgin Mary! Amen.

The above prayer is attributed to Blessed Hermann von Reichenau, a badly crippled but brilliant monk who died in 1054.

Memorare

Remember, O most gracious Virgin Mary, that never was it known, that anyone who fled to thy protection, implored thy help, or sought thy intercession was left unaided.
Inspired by this confidence, I (we) fly unto you, O Virgin of virgins, my mother; to thee do I (we) come, before thee I (we) stand, sinful and sorrowful. O

Mother of the Word Incarnate, despise not my (our) petitions, but in thy mercy hear and answer me. Amen.

This prayer is attributed to St. Bernard of Clairvaux, 12th century.

Ways of praying the rosary

The rosary can be a very free flowing conversation with God. It is framed by a few set prayers, but they form the background for meditation, which is an open dialogue or conversation with the Lord.

Praying the rosary is relatively easy. If you know the four basic prayers, then you only need to know what are called the mysteries. There's nothing particularly mysterious about them; almost all of them are events taken directly from the Gospels. The idea of the rosary is to say the beads while thinking about the events in the Gospels. In reflecting on these mysteries, we can think about how Jesus and Mary felt as well as how they can be related to one's own life. What virtues or lessons can we learn from them? It takes a little practice. What follows is information for those who are not knowledgeable about the rosary. Those who are may wish to skip to the endnote.

The easiest way, if you haven't done it before, is to say the rosary with a group. Many if not most Catholic churches have a time for saying the rosary at one time or another during the week. One can also hear it said on radio. An easy way, with a computer, is to look up "praying the rosary" on You Tube.

What follows is the basic way of saying the rosary. The whole thing can be done in fifteen to twenty minutes or longer, and can even be said while driving a car, though I'd delay praying at intersections or in busy traffic. Beads, obtainable online or at any religious goods store, are definitely helpful, though one can also use fingers to count the prayers. However, beads blessed by a priest do entail extra graces, at least for Catholics.

Some people say the rosary at bedtime, and it frequently puts them to sleep. Someone said, was it Bishop Sheen? that the angels finish it for you. Others say the rosary or other prayers while taking a walk. Many people who wake up at night say the rosary, or only a decade or two on their fingers or on beads before they go back to sleep. The rosary is easy to say silently anytime.

One further note before presenting the full rosary. The meditations, or "mysteries," come directly from the Gospels, with one or two exceptions. They are listed below. Just knowing them is fine for starting. However, like anything, the more that one knows, the more one can get out of the meditations. For that reason, actually reading the Gospels, which are considerably less than 200 pages total, is helpful to understand the mysteries and provides material to think about when reciting the prayers. Alternatively, a short pamphlet on the rosary listing the mysteries can often be picked up from a rack in Catholic churches or in religious articles and book stores. Or, the information can be found easily on the internet.

Sign of the Cross
Apostles' Creed

☐ Our Father

▭ Hail Mary

▬ Glory Be

Hail Holy Queen
(to finish the Rosary)

Meditate on the
Mysteries while
praying each decade.

Finish

Start

Step by step complete basic rosary

(Joyful mysteries)
[*Make the sign of the cross*] In the name of the Father, the Son and the Holy Spirit.
By the way, with all the prayers, one can either say them aloud or pray them silently. They can be prayed with rosary beads or even on fingers.

The Apostles' Creed: I believe in God the Father Almighty, Creator of heaven and earth; and in Jesus Christ, His only Son, our Lord; Who was conceived by the Holy Spirit, born of the Virgin Mary, suffered under Pontius Pilate, was crucified, died and was buried. He descended into hell. On the third day He arose again; He ascended into heaven, and sits at the right hand of God, the Father Almighty; from thence He shall come to judge the living and the dead. I believe in the Holy Spirit, the holy Catholic (or universal) Church, the communion of saints, the forgiveness of sins, the resurrection of the body, and life everlasting. Amen.

The Our Father: [*If you have a rosary, now hold the first large bead nearest the cross.*] Our Father, who art in heaven, hallowed be Thy name. Thy kingdom come, Thy will be done on earth as it is in heaven. Give us this day our daily bread, and forgive us our trespasses as we forgive those who trespass against us. And lead us not into temptation, but deliver us from evil. Amen.

The Hail Mary: [*Moving one by one to the next three beads, say three Hail Marys.*] Hail Mary, full of grace, the Lord is with thee. Blessed art thou among women, and blessed is the fruit of thy womb, Jesus. Holy Mary, Mother of God, pray for us sinners, now and at the hour of our death. Amen.

Glory Be to the Father: [*Say this on the second large bead.*] Glory be to the Father, and to the Son and to the Holy Spirit. As it was in the beginning, is now and ever shall be, world without end. Amen.

Say the first mystery, The Annunciation, and The Our Father. [*Use the same large bead as for the Glory Be to the Father.*]

The Hail Mary: [*While thinking of the angel's annunciation to Mary of the coming of Jesus, say ten Hail Marys on the next ten beads.*]

That's all there is to the first decade, or first ten beads of the rosary. To say a complete rosary, follow through the same way, saying the Glory Be to The Father, the name of the second mystery, and the Our Father on the large bead before continuing with ten Hail Marys on the next ten beads. You may finish with the Hail Holy Queen prayer.

To give you all the information you need, if you are new to, or not completely familiar with the rosary, the mysteries are listed below. Typically, different scriptural events are remembered in the rosary on different days. The Joyful Mysteries are usually said on Mondays and Saturdays, the Sorrowful Mysteries on

Tuesday and Friday, the Glorious Mysteries on Wednesday and Sunday, and Luminous Mysteries on Thursdays. The idea is to vary the prayer through the week. If, however, Christmas falls on a Tuesday or Friday, the Joyful Mysteries are more appropriate than the Sorrowful Mysteries.

Joyful Mysteries

1. Annunciation of Angel Gabriel to Mary
2. Visit of Mary to Elizabeth
3. Birth of Jesus
4. Presenting Jesus in the temple
5. Finding twelve year old Jesus in the temple

The Sorrowful Mysteries

1. The agony in the garden
2. The scourging at the pillar
3. Soldiers mock and crown Jesus with thorns
4. Jesus carries his cross
5. Jesus is crucified

The Glorious Mysteries

1. Jesus rises from the dead
2. Jesus ascends into heaven
3. The Holy Spirit descends on Christ's followers
4. The Assumption of Mary into heaven
5. Mary crowned Queen of heaven

Luminous Mysteries

1. The baptism of Jesus in the River Jordan
2. The wedding at Cana, Christ's first miracle
3. Jesus proclaims the Kingdom of God
4. The Transfiguration of Jesus
5. The Last Supper and the Eucharist

The other mysteries of the rosary have been known since the Middle Ages, but the Luminous Mysteries were proclaimed by Pope John Paul II in 2002. Many people are not as familiar with them.

Chapter Twelve

A Unique Apparition

Following Mary's numerous and detailed apparitions at Fatima, we will consider only one more, another of the few with full Vatican approval. In some ways, it is unusual. I think you will see why.

Banneux, Belgium, 1933

Mary's appearance to the child of a family that rarely went to church may be atypical, but the power of Mary's message is clear. Mariette, the oldest of seven children, was approaching her twelfth birthday. Her father, Julian Beco, was an unemployed wire maker who hadn't been to church for years. They lived in a cramped four room house where, except for a small image of Mary, there was nothing of a religious nature.

Mariette Beco had been going to Catechism classes so she could receive Holy Communion, but her attendance was irregular and her progress was poor. However, one day she happened to find a rosary on the road, and she carried it with her everywhere.

On a cold, windy night, January 15th, 1933, Mariette looked out the window, concerned that her younger brother had still not returned. Being the oldest of the Beco children, she also kept an eye on the baby in a cradle. As she looked out the window, a young lady appeared a few yards away, beautiful and luminous. Mariette called to her mother. When her mother came, Mariette described to her what she was seeing. Her mother, seeing only a white glow, said, "Nonsense" and drew down the window curtain.

Mariette opened the curtain again and said, "She's beautiful, Mama. She's smiling at me!" Seeing that the Lady had a rosary, Mariette got hers out and began to pray. She saw Our Lady's lips moving, but she didn't hear anything. The Lady motioned for Mariette to come outside. Mariette rose to go to her, but her mother, who saw only a white glow, thought the vision could be something evil and she hastily locked the door. The girl returned to the window to look out and found that the Lady has disappeared.

Mariette went to school the next day and told a friend what happened. Her friend told her that she should tell the priest. They both headed toward Fr. Louis Jamin's office, but at the last minute Mariette backed out. However, on Wednesday evening she returns to her Catechism class and that night she does so well that Fr. Jamin is amazed.

That same evening, on January 18th, Mariette feels drawn outside. Going out, in the darkness she kneels down and begins to pray her rosary. Her father saw her there kneeling, seemingly impervious to the cold, and he contacts a neighbor who, with his twelve year old son, watch her. Mariette suddenly stretches out her arms when she sees Mary appear in the distance until Mary stands only a short distance from her, also moving her lips in prayer. For about twenty minutes they pray together, and then Mary motions for Mariette to follow her.

Quickly running to the nearby road, she is led to a small spring of water, where she is told, "Put your hands into the water." She does this and Mary says to her, **"This spring is reserved for me."** Then she adds, **"Good night and we'll meet again."**

Late that night, Father Jamin and another priest visit the Beco house. Mariette is asleep and they talk with her father, who, while not seeing the apparition, witnessed his daughter's actions. Father Jamin is surprised when he learns that Mr. Beco wants to go to confession and return to the Church.

Word is starting to get out about the apparition. The next evening, wearing her father's old overcoat over her head because of the cold, Mariette kneels down in the snow. She is surrounded by seventeen people including her father. Soon Mary appears, and Mariette stretches out her hands, saying, "There she is!" There was silence until Mariette asked, "Who are you, beautiful lady?" Her answer was, **"I am the Virgin of the poor."**

The Virgin then led her again to the spring where she said, **"This spring is reserved for all the nations, to bring comfort to the sick."** Mariette repeated her words clearly and then quite spontaneously said, "Thank you! **Thank you!"** Mary told her, **"I will pray for you; good bye for now."**

The next evening, the night of the fourth apparition, Mariette did not feel well, but went outside anyway and began to say the rosary. Thirteen witnesses were there, including her parish priest, Father Jamin. When Our Lady appeared, Mariette asked her, "Beautiful Lady, what are your wishes?" Mary answered, "**I would like a small chapel built.**" With her right hand, she traced the sign of the cross over Mariette's head. Then, due to her sickness and the cold, the girl passed out. Her father and his neighbor carried the girl inside where she regained consciousness and then went to sleep peacefully in her bed.

In the following weeks Mariette didn't see anything of Mary, though she continued to go out each evening to kneel down and pray the rosary. She would go the short distance to the little spring that Mary had pointed out to her where with a few others she would say rosaries. Mary appeared to her next on the evening of the eleventh of February and told her, "**I have come to relieve suffering. I shall see you again soon.**"

Mariette received three more apparitions of Our Lady that winter. Mary's words in those meetings were not long. On her sixth appearance she said, "**Believe in me, and I will believe in you. Pray very much, goodbye for now.**" Her words on the seventh appearance were, "**My dear child, pray, pray very much.**" On her eighth and last apparition, Mary said, "**I am the Mother of the Savior, the Mother of God. Pray very much. Adieu, till we meet in God.**"

This time, Mary used the word adieu, which in French is a complete goodbye, such that there would be no further visions. Heartbroken, Mariette sobbed, knowing she would never see Our Lady again until heaven.

Miraculous healings at the spring and the conversion of many who had been lukewarm or even not practicing their faith continued. Mariette wanted to remain unknown, and unlike Sister Lucia of Fatima, she did not write about her experiences or the apparitions of the Blessed Virgin. Consequently, little is known about her life. She married during the second World War, a salesman, one account has it, they had three children, and divorced. Why there was a divorce is not known. In 2008, she made a statement about the apparitions. "I was no more than a postman who delivers the mail. Once this is done, the postman is of no importance any more."

Mariette always shunned publicity. She lived most of her life near where she grew up, and was close to her surviving son and daughter and her grandchildren. Even in her later years, she would quietly visit the spring where a chapel was erected—the place where Mary had appeared to her. On December 2nd, 2011, at the age of ninety, Mariette died, fittingly at the Residence La Vierge des Pauvres, or, in English, Home of the Virgin of the Poor. The care center is named after Mary's words at the third apparition of Banneux, **"I am the Virgin of the poor."** Now, Mariette is at last with her beloved Virgin.

Because Mariette wanted to live a private life, unlike many of those who witnessed apparitions, she did not become a religious or otherwise separate herself from ordinary people. She married, had children, and for unknown reasons her marriage ended in divorce. Her devotion to Mary, one she learned at the age of eleven, remained strong throughout her life. That Mary chose this young peasant girl to deliver her message says much about how God works through ordinary people.

Photo of Mariette Beco and her brother

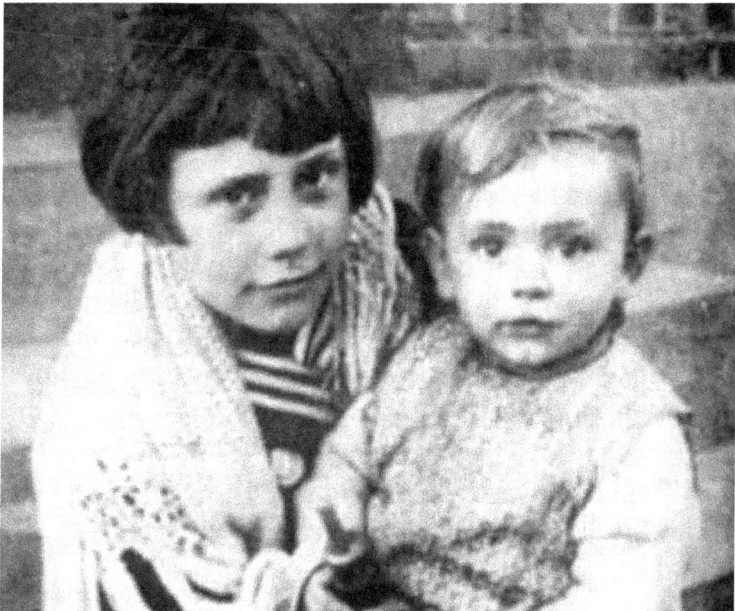

More recent apparitions

There have been other apparitions since 1933, and one of them has received full Vatican approval. The one in 1981 in Kibeho, Rwanda, Africa was approved by the bishop, and has since received the approval of Pope Francis who has encouraged devotion to Our Lady of Kibeho.

Surprisingly, the Marian sightings at Medjugorje, a town in former communist Yugoslavia, now Bosnia-Herzegovina, has not received the approval of the local bishop, which is normally the first step in getting Vatican approval. Nevertheless, the reported apparitions have been going on for six witnesses since 1981. Those teenagers are now middle aged, and most are married with children. Some still receive visions of Mary though not everyday as before. In 2024, the Vatican approved devotion to "Our Lady of Medjugorje granting a nihil obstat to her reverence without endorsing the apparitions themselves. Each month, Mary gives one of the visionaries a message to the world which is subsequently reported online and in many Catholic publications. An example, below is the one for November, 2025

Message, November 25, 2025

"Dear Children!
In this time of grace, I am calling you to follow me. Pray for those who do not pray and do not want peace and joy, which only the Most High can give. May your

souls be united in the joy of expectancy and your heart will be filled with peace. You will be convinced, little children, that all will be good and that God will bless all; because the good that you give will return to you, and joy will enfold your heart because you are with God and in God. Thank you for having responded to my call."

Medjugorje remains popular. Today, as many as two million people visit the site annually.

If you liked this book, consider giving it 4 or 5 stars on the book's page on Amazon. This actually helps the book come up when people are looking for similar kinds of books. To do so, scroll down on the left side of the book's page and you'll see an elongated circle where you can add stars and a review. A few words are enough. It's completely anonymous unless you want to give your name. Thank you! (Unfortunately, if you don't use Amazon for any purchases, it doesn't recognize you.)

Recent Nonfiction

Jesus, Kind, Loving, Dangerous

JESUS
KIND, LOVING,
DANGEROUS
Tom Molnar

The Pharisees realized right away that Jesus was a dangerous man. He was breaking their religious laws and keeping company with sinners. Ultimately, they had him crucified.

We, however, often get the watered down version of Jesus depicted in books and movies. He doesn't seem dangerous to us, but he is. His life changing message is not one of following laws, but of transforming hearts.

Time Out for Happiness

Not everyone grows up in a happy home with loving parents. I didn't. Today, most of us don't experience enough happiness in our daily lives. Anyone can feel downhearted. The key is knowing the ways to overcome our sadness.

Increasing happiness is much easier if we know how.

Time Out
For
Happiness

"in all our troubles, my joy overflows" (Paul)

Tom Molnar

Time Out for Happiness delivers insightful thinking on how to minimize sadness and increase joy. It features quick pick me ups as well as longer term strategies. Once we discard the ways that don't bring happiness and focus on those that do, like sharing with others, we will be well on our way to living a happier life. The truths found in this book are affirmed by those who have spent much of their working lives finding real answers to what brings happiness and joy.

The Universe of God and Humanity

Start with Adam and Eve and add evolution—two different stories or do they come together? Then add the discoveries that even Einstein couldn't believe, ones that have now quietly become a fact of life. Discoveries that have the power to change our view of God and the universe.

Already, the unexpected power of quantum mechanics is being used in our everyday lives, in cell phones, in lasers and at store checkout counters. What are the strange qualities of matter that can change how we look not only at the universe but also God and creation?

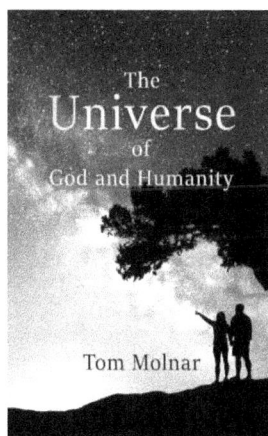

The
Universe
of
God and Humanity

Tom Molnar

Wired for Love

We all need love, from the strongest man to the most delicate woman. Young children, without love, are likely to die. All evidence shows that we human beings are genetically "hard wired" to give and receive love. In its absence, studies show that we tend to die sooner and experience far less happiness in our lives.

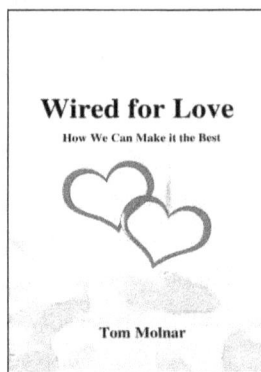

Wired for Love
How We Can Make it the Best

Tom Molnar

All titles are available on Amazon

The Crisis of Christianity
The Turning Point

Why have people walked away from church? Why do many children of faith-filled parents not attend services? Why do many parents today feel the need to protect their children from the negative influences of society?

Though we live in a time of change, surveys show that most people still believe in God. Even those who seldom or never attend religious services often maintain some prayer life and devotion. Nevertheless, it is undeniable that in Europe and much of the United States churches are closing and the number of Christians attending services is declining.

Why? This book will describe what has been happening in our culture and in our lives that has turned many away from their religious heritage. And yet, going forward, there is hope for the future.

Fiction

Swept Away

Swept Away draws from Civil War records, from accounts of life in the times, and from a true love story. It brings to life the story of Jenny, a girl turning 18 as the war begins. It finds her caught up in the love of a man for whom she is only his "best friend."

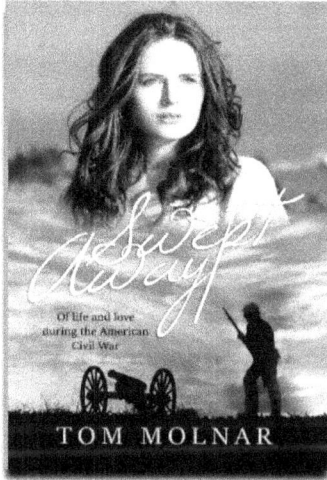

When Daniel leaves to fight for the South, Jenny's small town and her father's farm are soon occupied by hated Yankee soldiers. One of them, a Union captain, has the audacity to smile at her.

As the war intensifies, Jenny will find courage to do things she never thought she would do, and she will see things she never thought she would see.

Swept Away brings home the reality of war as well as life as it was lived in rural America. It is Jenny's story, one of love, the unexpected, and beginning anew.

Endnote—Practicalities

The rosary is the prayer form that Mary in so many of her public apparitions asked her followers to pray. While its format is much the same for everyone, each person's meditations and thoughts are their own whether saying the rosary alone or in a group. This is efficacious. Each of us live in our own personal environment, with different people, different jobs, different states in life, and different joys and concerns.

When the prayers of the rosary are mentally or vocally recited, the general focus is on the different mysteries, that is, events in the life of Christ, etc. Another focus can be the individual prayers of Hail Marys, Our Fathers, etc. However, very few of us, perhaps only saints, are able to completely take ourselves away from the concerns of our life. Our own thoughts enter in. During these times, we often get new insights from God. I might remember a friend or relative in need of prayers, or even that it has been a while since I called my mother. I might realize that I need to make amends with a person important in my life. Or, that there is something I should not forget to do. Certainly, the rosary is an excellent time to ask for a favor or make a request. It is also a wonderful time to enjoy being present in prayer with Our Lord and His mother, Mary.

Sometimes, one catches oneself simply daydreaming, and realizes that the current mystery has been forgotten. God understands our limitations and so does Our Lady. We are human, subject to all kinds of distractions, and may only need to try a little harder. Regardless, distractions will sometimes occur. God is aware of our intent, which may be more important than anything else.

The devil may try to lead one to believe that the rosary is a waste of time. "Give it up," the evil spirit will try to tell us. But don't be fooled. The rosary is a most efficacious prayer, especially as it includes the basic prayers of Christianity. Even if one has only enough time to say a decade or two, it is enough to thwart the evil one and can certainly help with salvation.

Limited Bibliography

The main source for Mary is scripture. However, these books stand out for me, providing additional information and perspective.

Henri Daniel-Rops, *Daily Life in the Time of Jesus.* This is a classic for understanding life in biblical times. Covers all facets of Jewish life. First copyright, 1961.

Arthur Klinck, *Everyday Life in Bible Times.* Another classic on the subject, now in its third or fourth edition. The short book gives one a real feel for the day to day life of biblical people–what they ate, how they dressed, their occupations, their homes, preparing food, etc. etc. First edition 1947.

Scot McKnight, *The Real Mary, Why Evangelical Christians Can Embrace the Mother of Jesus.* A heartfelt and down to earth telling of the story of Mary from an evangelical perspective. Copyright, 2007.

David Mills, *Discovering Mary, Answers to Questions About the Mother of God.* For anyone who would like to know the belief of the Catholic Church regarding almost every aspect of Mary, this book has the answers. Copyright, 2009.

Fulton J Sheen, *The World's First Love.* Older Christians remember Bishop Sheen from his sparkling TV shows where he shed light on many topics of Christianity. This is his eloquent book on Mary. Copyright 1952.

.

Acknowledgments

It would be remiss not to give credit to the artist. The cover painting is the work of a sixteenth century artist, Giovanni Battista Salvi, an Italian painter who lived in the Papal States. Born in 1609, he was active until his death in 1685. Much of Salvi's work focused on religious paintings which became more in demand following the Protestant Reformation. Consequently, besides his original paintings, he spent much of his time making copies of many of his most popular paintings for clients who sought his work. The back cover art is the work of French artist, Adolphe Jourdan. Born in Nimes, France in 1825, he exhibited in Paris and in 1876, in New York. He was renowned for his genre scenes and his portraits. He died in 1889.

Credit should also be given to my wife, whose practical advice is often spot on, as well as friends and relatives whose interest and perusal of the book have helped to improve the final edition.